# THE
# BASICS
# BOOK

*of OSI and Network Management*

# MOTOROLA UNIVERSITY PRESS

**The Motorola Codex Basics Book Series**
*The Basics Book of Information Networking*
*The Basics Book of X.25 Packet Switching*
*The Basics Book of ISDN*
*The Basics Book of OSI and Network Management*
*The Basics Book of Frame Relay*

# THE BASICS BOOK

*of OSI and Network Management*

Motorola Codex

**MOTOROLA
UNIVERSITY
PRESS**

**STEVE KU**

Addison-Wesley Publishing Company
Reading, Massachusetts   Menlo Park, California   New York
Don Mills, Ontario   Wokingham, England   Amsterdam
Bonn   Sydney   Singapore   Tokyo   Madrid   San Juan
Paris   Seoul   Milan   Mexico City   Taipei

The publisher offers discounts on this book when ordered in quantity for special sales.

For more information, please contact:
Corporate & Professional Publishing Group
Addison-Wesley Publishing Company
One Jacob Way
Reading, Massachusetts 01867

ISBN: 0-201-56371-1

Text printed on recycled and acid-free paper.
4 5 6 7 8 9 10-CRW-97969594
Fourth printing, November 1994

# PREFACE

This book is designed for management information system (MIS) people, pros and amateurs alike, who want a quick yet accurate summary of network management (NM). What is it? Who should worry about it? And why?

We assume that you know a little, but probably not a lot, about data communications. (If you want to brush up on the basics, refer to the first book in this series: the *Basics Book of Information Networking*.) We also assume that you and your company have at least some experience with a network and that somebody—maybe you—has a notion that this network could be managed better. Whoever has that notion is probably right.

But network management is a big universe, full of products and processes, and this little book doesn't attempt to cover it all in depth. The Introduction explains where network management came from and points out the aspects that will probably interest you. Chapter 1 defines the broad field of network management and gives an overview of the basic choices that a potential user faces. Chapter 2 describes different communications realms and how management takes place within and across them. Chapter 3 is a brief excursion into Open Systems Interconnection (OSI) and the other kinds of standards that come to bear on network communications. And finally, Chapter 4 puts all of this good knowledge to use, with scenarios for real-life network management.

One suggestion: if you want just a quick introduction to what network management is about, try reading Chapter 4 first. Then, inspired by how logical and accessible NM is, you may want to go back to the earlier chapters for some background. Or, if you come to this book as a fully motivated student of network management, read the chapters in sequence, and consider Chapter 4 your dessert for eating a good dinner in Chapters 1 through 3.

# TABLE OF CONTENTS

# INTRODUCTION

Once upon a time, there were no networks. Men in white lab coats stood behind glass partitions, and—through a slot in the door—accepted requests for data processing from their intimidated colleagues. These men worked in Central Computing: the center of the universe. You could tell it was the center of the universe because it had no windows.

Slowly, slowly, access was dispersed. Central Computing became the pooled computer resource, and so-called dumb terminals spread across the land—the local ones hard-wired directly into a mainframe and the remote ones connected via a modem and a leased-line telephone. (Most were local and hard-wired.)

Now there was shared access. Life was becoming more complicated. The computer, formerly a black box, was now an octopus with ever more numerous arms. This was threatening to the men in the lab coats, but still nothing much went wrong. And if something *did* go wrong, the fault was probably in one of those hard-wired arms. So problems, when they did occur, were usually easy to find and fix.

This remained true even after the development of minicomputers, which began to be distributed around the various departments of a given company. A minicomputer was a smaller, somewhat more flexible species of octopus, and it could be found in many more places— but it was still an octopus.

Then however, leased lines began to stand in for hard-wired cables, and a new kind of rough beast was born. This was the WAN, or wide area network. Suddenly, companies faced the challenge of network management. This was because WANs presented wholly new kinds of problems. For example: Who was responsible for planning and designing this new thing called a network? (This was different from modifying a generic octopus for installation at a particular site!) And how were changes in the network—as new equipment was installed and circuits rented—going to be planned, implemented, and documented? Could the network ever overcome the nasty, chronic incompatibility of devices made by different vendors? And what about security across the far-flung empire?

And then the local area network, or LAN, began to crawl out of the walls (literally, in some cases). LANs begin as islands—a way to give a group of more or less isolated users access to shared resources (printers and file-servers) in order to use those resources more efficiently, to facilitate the addition or relocation of terminals, and to give that isolated group of users at least some access to each other's work and applications.

You can guess what happened next: those isolated user groups began to look for ways to overcome their isolation. Now the WAN began to play a new and broader role, serving as a means of connecting LANs to each other and in some cases to a centralized computer resource.

This brings us to the present and to today's definitions of the wide area network. Question #1: What do you have when you have a central information system (IS) department (or perhaps several mainframe sites), lots of leased lines, and users spread out across multiple corporate offices? Answer: a WAN. Question #2: What do you have when you have one or more LANs reporting back to a central location or to multiple data centers? Again, a WAN.

WANs are direct descendents of the octopus with arms described earlier. They first flourished when multiplexers began to address the problem of high-priced, dedicated phone lines. Today, WANs include intelligent modems, multiplexers, T1/E1 processors, X.25 switches and PADS, ISDN gateways, and other equipment. In part because of the breakup of the phone company, the WAN is increasingly important in terms of network management.

By their nature, WANs find themselves in the middle of things. They are very likely to be what *you* will eventually focus on as you identify and solve your company's network management problems. It should come as no surprise, then, that WANs are what this book will eventually focus on.

This will require, first, a quick tour of the world of network management. Then we'll explore a little theory.

But don't be alarmed at the prospect. Motorola Codex has been a leader in network management for more than a decade, and in data communications for 30 years. Because we have multitechnology experience, we are network management specialists; thus, we can help you better understand WANS, LANs, and other unknowns.

# DEFINING NETWORK MANAGEMENT OR

*What's going on out there?*

What's in a network, and how do you manage one?

The simplest network consists of four types of hardware: terminals, also known as Data Terminal Equipment (DTEs); transmission devices such as modems or data service units (DSUs), also known as data communications equipment (DCEs); telephone lines; and a central processing unit (CPU). Of course, lots of other interesting pieces can be added. But without at least these four components and the software required to run them, you don't have a network.

Twenty years ago, if you called yourself a network specialist, you were most likely a hired gun. You were someone who designed, installed, and coaxed into operation a communications system consisting of some combination of these four pieces. Equally likely in those days, you called IBM to supply the computer, and you arranged to rent a few of AT&T's many, many phone lines. (We assume you called Motorola Codex for the modems.) You hooked everything up, flipped the switch, ran the necessary tests, and then you departed, applause in your ears, heading for that next big installation. Assuming that you were conscientious, you left behind a three-ring binder describing what you had done.

What happened after you left? Well, in most cases, life just kept getting more complicated. The network grew, was modified, and was modified again. To no one's surprise, problems cropped up. A full-time data communications manager was hired. He or she may have spent many hours puzzling over your three-ring binder: Why didn't things seem to match up any more?

Network trouble-shooting went from being an off-peak hobby to a high-stakes priority. But the overall approach to problem solving remained informal. In response to a complaint from Somewhere Out There, Corporate MIS might call the marooned user and suggest that she "throw switch 5." If that didn't work, Corporate might get back on the line with another suggestion such as, "Turn your terminal on and off a few times."

Out in the real world, meanwhile, all the component parts of the network evolved, often along independent paths. Chip and line technologies went through a series of transformations and so did the products based on them. Modems, for example, got smarter, meaning that they acquired the ability to run some basic diagnostic tests on the operations of the network. The datacomm manager, grateful for any solid clues, soon got accustomed to studying the indicator lights on those modems. What was going *on* out there?

A second external wildcard also emerged. In most cases, the network depended in part on leased lines, and the tariff structures that determined the cost of these lines were changeable. The pressure of technological developments combined with the variable tariffs posed new challenges for datacomm managers.

Meanwhile, back on the network, there was still trouble. As users grew more dependent on their machines, datacomm's phone calls—announcing users' inability to access the host from particular terminals—grew more irate. The manager would start calling in all the vendors responsible for one or more pieces of the troubled communications link. Did the problem belong to the terminal manufacturer? To the modem supplier? Or was it a problem in the phone line? (What was going *on* out there?) Eventually—not before several tense hours had gone by—teams of technicians with impressive test equipment would arrive. Sometimes they would isolate and fix the problem. Other times they would simply blame it on the other guy and go home. Fingerpointing was big.

Meanwhile, Corporate was beginning to think about this whole operation differently. It was one thing to have the network go down back in the days of Nixon, moon shots, and miniskirts when many companies still viewed the computing function as largely a prestigious, mysterious sideshow. But now—10, 15 years later—things were different. Competition had intensified. Computing and the information derived from it had moved to center stage. Computers, as it turned out, could make money for you. In this context, confusion, fingerpointing, and excuses were unacceptable. And even though downtime was more and more likely—the network was getting more complicated, and the equipment within that network wasn't getting any younger—downtime was less and less tolerable. A new approach was definitely needed.

To complicate things further, most of the vital links in that network, including the highly trained personnel who ran it and the data lines that carried information to and fro, had become much more expensive. Ten-year projections of network growth began to look horrendous: "At this rate of growth, not only will we have to buy four hundred more terminals, rent four dozen more printers, and lease another thirty phone lines, we'll also have to hire five more people in Corporate to beef up the MIS staff and another two or three people in Computer Maintenance and Support"—and so on, and so on.

In fact, as the strategic planners soon realized, there were really only three choices as they contemplated ways of managing an increasingly valuable and expensive resource: (1) add people to continue tending to the growing network at the established level of care (or greater), (2) stop tending to the growing network at that level of care, or (3) find a new technology that might complement the datacomm managers.

## A FIRST STEP: NETWORK CONTROL

In the mid-1970s, leading modem vendors (including, of course, Motorola Codex) began offering tools for testing network functions and diagnosing problems. Building on the capabilities of the smart modems that the datacomm manager had come to treasure, these tools consisted of a central device that communicated with all compatible modems in the network. This "shadow network" sent and received its signals over the same phone lines that

The 3000 Hz bandwidth can be split to accommodate a narrow secondary channel to carry network control command signals.

figure 1

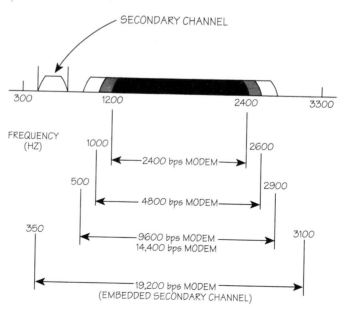

were used for transmitting "real" data. How? by means of a technique call **time division multiplexing (TDM)**, which creates a second, low-speed data channel alongside the main data channel.

This was a big step forward. These new tools—generally known as **network control systems (NCS)**—gave datacomm managers their first comprehensive look at their networks. And because these newfound diagnostic capabilities tended to produce clear indications of where a problem lay, fingerpointing among vendors was greatly reduced. *Availability* of the network was therefore enhanced.

Diagnosis, then, was a key function of the NCS. But what about control? In fact, a subset of these network control systems delivered what they promised: the ability to control the network by solving problems from the central location. Sometimes this involved a simple intervention, such as changing from one piece of equipment to a backup device. At other times, it involved a long-distance reconfiguration, or reprogramming, of a troublesome component in the network.

Again, this was good stuff, and the customers liked it. To no one's surprise, the giant mainframe manufacturers took steps to avoid getting left behind. IBM, for one, followed a slightly different route from the modem manufacturers. Big Blue already had a major investment in diagnostics for its central computers, and these diagnostics were based on a scheme whereby control signals were tucked into the main data channel along with the user's data stream. So when IBM extended its network control capabilities outward from its mainframes and front-end processors, it kept this original design, rather than going the multiplexing route. (More on this in a following section and also in Chapter 2.)

However, none of these NCS schemes was perfect. Although they handled modems more or less adequately, they didn't necessarily deal with other network components: multiplexers, switches, and so on. Furthermore, their user interfaces tended to be clunky and unfriendly. On a bad day, you might still hear that mournful cry echoing down the halls: "What's going *on* out there?" And because the systems were awkward to use, they tended not to be used enough. For example: if adding new network devices to the control system's registry hardware was cumbersome, well, maybe it didn't get done.

It was just as troubling that these network control systems were designed mainly to help users *react* to problems. They weren't very good at analyzing how whatever had just happened fit in with the larger picture. They were of little use in spotting a minor problem, such as a slowly degrading phone line, before it turned into a major problem. They couldn't spot and flag the subtle, submerged operational trends that sometimes turn out to be problems in the making.

Clearly, a new and more sophisticated generation of network control devices was needed. In the mid-1980s, this new generation began to emerge with a new name: **network management systems (NMS).**

## NETWORK MANAGEMENT TODAY

Network management today comprises four principal tasks: planning, building, maintaining, and improving a communications network from a central site.

NM helps achieve two crucial and mutually dependent goals: *higher network availability* and *network cost efficiency.* If you wanted to be absolutely sure of total network availability at all times, you'd station an around-the-clock body—live, smart, and expensive—and a pile of spare parts at every device and circuit in the network. Conversely, if you wanted to run the lowest-cost network, you'd never put a live body anywhere, ever—you'd put the whole thing on automatic pilot. Both availability and efficiency are highly desirable, but neither of the extreme solutions just outlined is feasible. Network management is a sophisticated way of splitting the difference.

Today's NMS incorporates all of the features of yesterday's NCS, but it also adds a management database element. Sounds innocent enough—a "management database element"—but in fact, this distinction is a major one. Why? Because by drawing on a database consisting specifically of data for the entire network, the NMS can organize, analyze, and predict network faults and trends. It can truly answer the question, "What's going *on* out there?"

Three more things must be said in this overview of the contemporary art of network management. First, the initial two tasks stated above—planning and building—tend to imply that the user is starting from scratch. If you are, well, lucky you. But most often in the real world, a managed network is heterogeneous, meaning simply that its various bits and pieces have come at different times from different vendors. Especially in light of the sustained binge of mergers and acquisitions that took place in the 1980s, this has become an ever more important part of the NM challenge.

Second, network management has traditionally implied the existence of a large network. (For argument's sake, let's say a large network is one with hundreds, rather than dozens, of lines or circuits) Until recently, the relatively high cost of network management has had to be spread over a large network. But more options, including relatively inexpensive systems, are becoming available today. Some of these systems, moreover, are upgradeable, enabling the user to add sophisticated and more expensive capabilities only when they are needed.

And third, again in the real world, all of these activities overlap, and none of them ever really stops. Planning and improving a network may sound like the logical first and last steps in a sequence, but life is rarely that simple. Network management today is two things: a product (a collection of hardware and software) and a process (management of that collection, and the people who oversee it). Because the product keeps evolving, the management process never stops.

Which leads us, finally, to an unexpected piece of advice from a manufacturer of network management systems. If you're going to put your emphasis anywhere, put it on the *process*. It's even pronounced that way: network *management*.

## THE "GOOD" NMS

Assuming that you're starting from scratch—again, lucky you!—you should be interested in building a number of features into your NMS. We'll look at NMS functions at some length in Chapters 3 and 4, but for now, we can summarize the operations of a "good" NMS in three words: performance, accessibility, and integration.

**Performance** is an umbrella for a number of criteria. How fast does the system report events, perform tests, and generate reports? How many users can it support? How many devices can it handle?

**Accessibility** essentially means ease of use. How user friendly is the system? Does it have a consistent user interface, database, inventory mechanism, and alarm reporting and control scheme for all network components? Does it have enough flexibility so that you can monitor the network by location, device type, application, or other criteria? Does it provide interfaces to systems that do what it doesn't?

After you define the operations you want your NMS to perform, how **integrated** do you want those operations to be? In other words, is the system intelligent enough to appropriate the information used in one management application for use in another application? For example, will the system automatically incorporate information uploaded from a new device into the system's inventory database? Because the alternative is lots of laborious keystroking—that is, many opportunities for errors of omission and commission—most companies quickly respond yes to this question and others like it. (We're considering here one kind of integration; we'll discuss another—integration across multiple technologies—in the next chapter.)

Clearly, there are also other concerns: ease of migration, upgradeability, security, and more. We'll have more to say about all of these issues in the pages that follow.

## MORE NMS CHOICES

Performance, accessibility, and integration are the datacomm equivalent of mom and apple pie. (Once people get the concept, in other words, they'd have to be crazy not to support them.) So the real question for most people isn't, Do I want these good things? Instead, the real question is, How much of each of these good things does my budget allow me to get? But there are a couple of other choices—and related terminology—that aren't so obvious, and with which the current and potential NMS user needs to be familiar. Let's look briefly at several alternative ways of slicing the network management pie. They are: CPU-based versus freestanding NMS, and logical versus physical NMS.

Earlier, we mentioned that the mainframe computer manufacturer's approach to NM has been to "grow" NM capabilities outward from the CPU. IBM, for example, has developed a **System Network Architecture (SNA)** that attempts to allow all aspects of network management to be performed from the host computer. In theory, it's a sensible approach. You already have a big, powerful computer sitting there, working hard for all those people across your network. Why not ask it to work just a little harder and take on the NM function?

Unfortunately, life tends to be more complicated than that. To begin with, CPU manufacturing is simply not specialized in this area. So even if you were starting from scratch with the opportunity to build in NM from the beginning, there's almost no chance that you could design a CPU-based NM system that would be as flexible as a specialized manager.

On the other hand, a specialized or freestanding NMS doesn't attempt to take over the internal management functions of the CPU, because IBM and other computer manufacturers have consistently performed that task very well. Again, the important measure is integration. Whatever else your NMS does, it has to integrate easily and effectively with all the other systems with which you do business.

The second major distinction, **logical** versus **physical NM,** is a variation on this same theme. IBM's approach, described previously, can be considered a logical NM scheme. Logical NM focuses on the logical components of the network—in other words, the applications. It allows the systems operator to ask and answer questions such as, How are my applications doing in my network? How many users are accessing them? What sessions are going on throughout the network right now? Logical NM allows the operator to see problems in the network and begin diagnosing them. Physical NM slices the pie quite differently. It focuses on the physical components of the network. It allows the datacomm manager to ask and answer questions such as, Are all the modems, switches, multiplexers, lines, and so on in my network functioning adequately?

And why is *this* helpful? Because when a problem arises with a given piece of equipment, there are often ways to diagnose and repair it quickly and in the meantime reroute data traffic around the problem.

Motorola Codex, among other leading designers and vendors of freestanding NMSs, has focused on physical management. Why? Because that's our area of expertise. But we're not dogmatic about it. In fact, being versatile, highly connectible, and realistic, we are always happy to build all the necessary bridges to our logical siblings in network management.

## THE SHAPE OF CHAPTERS TO COME

So much for introductions, definitions, and choices.

We have stated that network management today consists of four principal tasks: planning, building, maintaining, and improving a communications network. That's true; and it's probably what interests you most. In Chapter 4, we will return to these challenges, and examine some real-life scenarios of network management in action.

First, though, we need to consider some concepts and theories in Chapters 2 and 3. It's a necessary voyage, and we will try to make it entertaining.

## WHEN
## WORLDS
## COLLIDE
## OR

WANs, LANs, and SuperMans

This chapter concerns those areas of an information network that require some kind of management. We'll call them "operational worlds." There are four or five of them depending on how you subdivide the information networking universe: data processing/management information systems (DP/MIS), telephony, wide area networking (WAN), and local area networking (LAN). Finally, there's the LAN-interconnect universe, which you can think of either as part of the LAN world or as a self-contained cosmos. In any case, these worlds can be mapped as follows:

**DP/MIS,** of course, has always been the center of the data-processing action. This is the home of main-frames and minicomputers, remote cluster controllers, windowless rooms, and so forth. This is where most of your MIS money has probably been going for years. This is the resource to which every user wants cheap, dependable, and

An information network can be divided into five operational worlds, each of which requires some kind of management.

figure 2

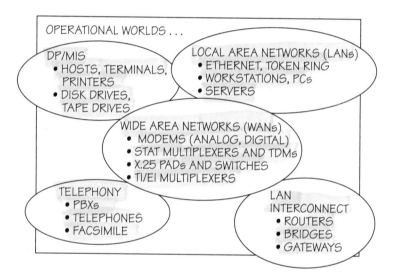

easy access. Most likely, that need for access is the primary reason why you're reading this book. Enough said about DP/MIS.

And then, there's **telephony** (accent on the second syllable.) Here's where you fax, phone, and generally move voice and data around, most often using specialized phone equipment in the context of a private branch exchange (PBX). Long the exclusive domain of the phone company, the telephony world has been opened wide as a result of divestiture. And that's probably another reason you're reading this book. It used to be that we could leave the management of our networks to Ma Bell. No longer! She has checked out, and left much of her luggage and many of her former responsibilities behind. We now have many options, and have to make our own decisions.

We've already introduced the notion of **local area networks (LANs)**. This is the newest of the worlds. LANs allow a variety of equipment to share such resources as storage devices and printers; to swap files; to communicate via electronic mail; and to otherwise share and exchange information. LANs have helped overcome some of the difficulties associated with the old octopus-with-arms computer network: slow response times, limited expansion capabilities, nightmarish, spaghetti-like tangles of wires, and so on.

LANs were once thought of mainly as isolated islands. Increasingly, though, the isolated LAN is getting hooked up to something, and the growing need for greater connectivity has prompted the development of **LAN interconnection** devices. That means exactly what it says: these devices link LANs, whether in the same building or different states, to allow all those good sharings and exchanges to go on. LAN interconnects can be bridges, routers, or gateways. We won't go into detail here, but you should be aware that these LAN interconnects are sometimes considered their own world.

Saving the best for last, we have the **wide area network (WAN)**, the center of the NM action. Note how, with the benefit of a little creative cartography, our map of the operational-world universe in Figure 2 puts WANs not only in the *middle* of everything, but also slightly *overlapping* all the other worlds. WANs tie it all together, linking nations and continents, LANs and hosts and PBX terminals, and just about every other productive hook-up you can think of. They do this with the help of modems, DSUs, high-speed T1/E1 multiplexers, X.25 PADs and switches, and other combinations of hardware and software. WANs are—or should be—wonderful.

Each of these worlds has, over time, developed its own set of management tools. The management goal has been, first, to link the pieces used *within* each world, and, second and more problematic, to integrate management functions *across* worlds.

Although management of telephony and DP/MIS resources has traditionally been the province of the carriers and computer companies, respectively, companies specializing in network management have risen to the challenge of managing the LAN and WAN areas. **LAN managers,** as you'll surely guess, perform the NM function for the local area network. As suggested in the last chapter, many network topologies are gradually being transformed from hierarchical to flat. Both WANs and LANs have contributed to this evolution. Multiple LAN installations, for example, have gradually encroached on the turf of the centralized computing resource, and each of these installations is a potential site for LAN management.

At the same time, phone tariffs have been declining, so it's become increasingly tempting to hook up two or more LAN installations in a larger network. This is accomplished over a WAN, often by means of a LAN interconnect. As computer prices continue to drop by 15 or 20 percent per year, it seems clear that the desktop-to-desktop mesh network topology—similar to the telephone network—will become the most common network structure. This will lead, naturally, to a greater dependence on effective WAN management.

Which brings us to our second management world: **WAN managers.** WAN management assists in all the good processes that we earlier ascribed to WANs. WAN management ensures, for example, that traffic can flow to and from the host computer. It helps make sessions that are going on within a host (or hosts) available to terminals at the farthest reaches of the network. (DP/MIS management plays a role in this, too, of course. The difference is, as we've seen, that computer companies typically focus on logical management—the applications the network is running—rather than the physical components typically managed by WAN managers.) WAN management helps get voice traffic across T1/E1 boundaries in the telephony world. And finally, it serves to interconnect LAN installations and manage traffic among them.

This leads us naturally to the subject of *interfaces*. It is of course possible to design a LAN and an associated LAN management system that are absolutely self-contained. (It's been done.) This is something like building a railroad with a particular gauge track such that only the cars designed for that gauge track could use it.

This is also true for WANs. But because WANs are essentially big, fast railroads, it wouldn't make much sense to device a WAN management system without interfaces to other kinds of management systems—in other words, a sort of standard gauge. Motorola Codex is very much interested in interfaces and connectivity. It seems obvious to us that WAN managers in particular have to focus on how the boxcars are going to get from Railroad A to Railroad B. If, for example, the LAN manager is producing good information for the benefit of a larger network, of if that LAN manager is one that takes orders well from the larger network, the WAN manager should certainly take advantage of that good situation.

But why not go even further? Why not design a network management system that can do it all? This way of thinking led to the development of the so-called **SuperManagers,** designed and offered by the big computer companies and carriers. IBM, for reasons described in Chapter 1, has the longest-running claim on this territory. In 1986, it introduced a SuperManager called NetView, designed to take advantage of IBM's proprietary Systems Network Architecture (SNA) and provide end-to-end network management. At least in theory, NetView can reach to the ends of your network, sending and receiving management information to and from all kinds of devices and generally making things hum.

In practice, though, this system has its limits. Because IBM is a dominant player in some three-quarters of all large networks, most independent vendors have chosen to adopt the protocols that allow them to hook up with NetView. Even so, two-way NM communication through NetView (and its interface, NetView/PC) doesn't yet serve all the NM needs of a complex network. For example, NetView doesn't provide for the integrated NM database that we emphasized Chapter 1.

SNA is logical in orientation, meaning that it is focused primarily on applications rather than on the physical objects in the network. NetView provides good logical management, but its approach to physical management is relatively unsophisticated. Thus, as we'll see in Chapter 4, it sometimes makes sense to combine two NMSs: one aimed at logical management, and the other aimed at physical management.

Last but not least, running NetView full time takes a *lot* of mainframe capacity. Which is OK if you've got brainpower to spare or if you don't mind buying a little more brainpower.

AT&T has developed its own package of products and protocols labeled the Universal Network Management Architecture (UNMA). Taking advantage of UNMA is the Accumaster Integrator, AT&T's entry into the SuperManager field. The relative openness of UNMA, in contrast with the proprietary standards of Netview, is intended to help AT&T compete with IBM's huge installed base. (More on open and proprietary standards in the next chapter.) Unlike NetView, however, the Accumaster Integrator presupposes that complete and accurate information will be fed to it by DP/MIS, WAN, and LAN "element managers" (AT&T's term).

Digital Equipment Corporation, too, has entered the SuperManager field. Its architecture is Enterprise Management Architecture (EMA) and its SuperManager is the DECmcc Director. This product is an outgrowth of an unusual alliance of high-tech companies (whose seven original members include your NM tour guide, Motorola Codex). The Director, which facilitates the management of those seven companies' products, is more "peer-to-peer" oriented than the IBM and AT&T entries in the SuperManager field. In other words, it permits an exchange of information rather than establishing a hierarchical "master–slave" relationship. DEC is only the latest titan to enter the fray; more are sure to follow.

You might well be asking at this point, Are WAN managers and LAN managers doomed? In other words, is it only a matter of time before the King SuperManager emerges, omniscient and all-powerful, capable of every type of network intervention?

In a word, no. We're now entering the realm of trade-offs. It's great to keep things simple, and it's always tempting to turn all of law enforcement over to Superman. But the higher up the NM hierachy you go—into the reaches of the SuperManager, for example—the more difficult it becomes to provide specific NM features for every type of device. It's relatively easy to keep track of a particular printer on the LAN, or a particular T1/E1 node on the WAN, from the SuperManager. It's far more difficult to *manage* that printer or, T1/E1 node without a LAN or WAN manager as well—especially if that SuperManager is action oriented, rather than device oriented. It's like the levels of government: conducting the national census is a good task for the federal government, whereas conducting local voter registration is not.

*Integration* is, again, a key concept. As integration becomes more difficult, it tends to stop happening. And when your NM activities aren't integrated—when all the implications of a change in status of a device or circuit aren't logically linked within the NMS—those activities won't have the impact they should have.

The moral of the story, as we see it, is that no NMS can be all things to all networks. A good LAN manager is the best NMS for the LAN element (assuming, of course, that it communicates effectively with other element managers). Similarly, a good WAN manager is the undisputed champ of the WAN element, especially if it is very accomplished at helping other element managers (SuperManagers, LAN managers, telephony, and DP/MIS managers) talk to each other. Thus, a "peer-to-peer" relationship between element managers—including, where appropriate, a SuperManager—is often the best NM solution.

## TOO MANY SYSTEMS

Having made our pitch for complexity, we'll now make a case for simplicity.

For most companies in the real world, the question isn't, Should I go LAN manager, WAN manager, SuperManager, DP/MIS manager, telephony manager, or a particular combination of the above? Instead, the question is, Given where I am today, in terms of my network and applications, what network management system(s) do I need?

Most companies today are in chaos. In the case of a WAN, for example, a company may be enjoying the many benefits of a well-designed wide area network; or, it may be living with something more like a WAAHH (wide area accident, happened here). That is to say, at first one vendor was on the scene, providing network elements and some rudimentary means of controlling that stuff; then another came in with new stuff and a way of controlling *that* stuff; and then a third vendor came in, and so on, and so on. As Chairman Mao once said, "Let a hundred flowers bloom." And after enough time has passed, well, we're talking *lots* of different technologies and products, all throbbing away under one network "roof."

Maybe those separate vendors (probably under pressure from their shared client) found a way to mesh their network control systems together without sacrificing too much functionality. But when they didn't, they just ran their own pipe up to headquarters, provided a more or less clunky user NM interface, and checked out.

Eventually, this scenario leads us back to that pathetic image we evoked much earlier: of the datacomm manager staring at unrelated, unintegrated screens across a half-dozen management stations, wondering bleakly what was going *on* out there. Station One was reporting something about Technology A. Station Two was more or less diagnosing and controlling the state of Product B. Station Three, as far as anyone knew, was giving some sort of hint about Vendor C's datacomm product line. And so on, and so forth. Not a pretty sight.

We've already talked about the advantages of one kind of integration in the NM context—the integration of information into a common database that allows data resulting from one management application to be used in other applications. Now, we're introducing another type of integration—integration of network components under a common management system.

Integration! A consolidated view of the entire network! Problem determination and problem solving across the network! Increased life expectancies for datacomm managers around the world!

Exciting prospects, to which we'll return in Chapter 4. Meanwhile, how in the world will such integration be done?

## THE CASE FOR STANDARDS

Logically, if you wanted to tie all your NM components within a particular domain (LAN, WAN, or whatever) together, and if you wanted to tie together components across domain boundaries, you'd need the benefit of some sort of **standards** to which all of those components could adhere. The only alternative is lots of individual proprietary gateways, which not only adds expense but also makes the network more complicated when the whole point of network management is to *simplify* the process of overseeing and controlling the network.

The number of vendors that understand this is definitely on the rise, and the number of so-called "open systems" is proliferating. The definition of "open" varies from vendor to vendor, however. Some vendors combine their commitment to open standards with an open operating environment. Others are working to develop open interfaces that enable users to run applications between managers from different vendors. Hewlett-Packard, for example, has developed a management system called OpenView which users can customize for compatibility with other vendors' equipment.

It took the railroads decades to settle on standard gauges for track. Leading companies in the world of data communications (including Motorola Codex) hope we can do better. In fact, the process of standard-setting is already well under way, and the development and status of standards for network management are the subjects of Chapter 3.

**3**

# A HITCHHIKER'S GUIDE TO OSI
## OR

*thumbs up for standards*

This chapter features a gaggle of acronyms, almost none of them pronounceable.

To begin, there's a group called the ISO, the International Organization for Standardization. This group consists of representatives of the many constituencies within the wide world of data communications and telecommunications—from vendors to users to carriers. Among other things, the ISO has a committee working on a set of standards that will permit communication between different network management systems. This **Open Systems Interconnection (OSI)** Committee has developed a **Basic Reference Model** that describes an architecture in which overall data com-

The OSI Basic Reference Model subdivides overall data communications processes into seven functional layers.

munications activities are partitioned into seven functional layers (Figure 3).

Layers 1 through 3 (the *physical, data link,* and *network* layers) deal with getting data from Point A to Point B over a specific network technology (and,

**figure 3**

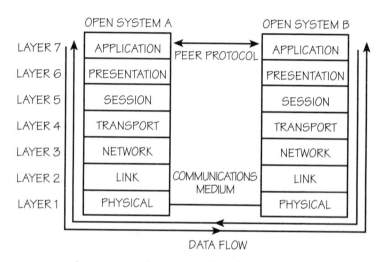

to a certain extent, also preparing the information for transport). Layers 4 through 7, in contrast, deal with communicating the data independent of the network used. The interface between adjacent layers standardizes access points so that hardware and software systems can be compatible with each other, regardless of manufacturer. Over the long run, this effort will make it possible for people to exchange data using products from multiple vendors, all of whom have made a commitment to *open* systems and standards, rather than *closed* (or *proprietary*) ones.

Each layer of the OSI Model performs a specific data communications task—a service to and for the layer that precedes it (e.g., the network layer provides a service for the transport layer). The process can be likened to placing a letter in a series of envelopes before it's sent through the postal system (Figure 4). Each succeeding envelope adds another layer of processing or overhead information necessary to process the transaction. Together, all the envelopes help make sure the letter gets to the right address and that the message received is identical to the message sent. Once the entire package is received at its destination, the envelopes are opened one by one until the letter itself emerges exactly as written.

In a datacomm transaction, however, each end user is unaware of the envelopes, which perform their functions transparently. For example, we can track an automatic teller machine (ATM) transaction through our multilayer system. One multiple layer system (Open

The OSI Basic Reference Model can be likened to placing a letter in a series of envelopes; each envelope bears information necessary to ensure the letter arrives at its proper address exactly as written. Once the letter reaches its destination, the envelopes are opened one by one, until the letter itself emerges.

figure 4

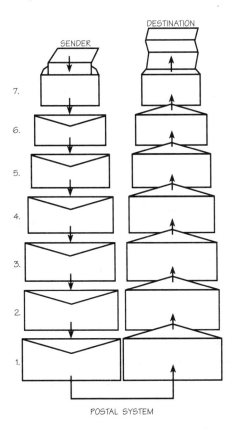

System A) provides an application layer that is an interface to the person attempting a transaction, while the other multiple layer system (Open System B) provides an application layer that interfaces with ATM applications software in the bank's host computer. The corresponding layers in Open Systems A and B are called peer layers and communicate through **peer protocols.** These peer protocols provide communication support for the user's application, performing transaction-related tasks such as debiting an account, dispensing currency, or crediting an account.

Actual data flow between the two open systems (Open System A and Open System B), however, is from top to bottom in one open system (Open System A, the source), across the communications line, and then from bottom to top in the other open system (Open System B, the destination). Each time user application data pass downward from one layer to the next in the same system, processing information is added. When that information is removed and processed by the peer layer in the other system, it causes various tasks (error correction, flow control, etc.) to be performed. You, the ATM user, are unaware of any of this, of course, but in fact that's what's happening while the words, "Please wait, your transaction is being processed" appear on the screen.

To date, the ISO has labored away on all seven layers, which are summarized below in the order in which the data actually flow as they leave the source:

- Layer 7, the *application* layer, provides for a user application (such as getting money from an ATM) to interface with the OSI application layer. That OSI application layer has a corresponding peer layer in the other open system, the bank's host computer.
- Layer 6, the *presentation* layer, makes sure the user information (a request for $50 in cash to be debited from your checking account) is in a format (i.e., syntax or sequence of ones and zeros) the destination open system can understand.
- Layer 5, the *session* layer, provides synchronization control of data between the open systems (i.e., makes sure the bit configurations that pass through layer 5

at the source are the same as those that pass through layer 5 at the destination).

- Layer 4, the *transport* layer, ensures that an end-to-end connection has been established between the two open systems (i.e., layer 4 at the destination "confirms the request for a connection," so to speak, that it has received from layer 4 at the source).
- Layer 3, the *network* layer, provides routing and relaying of data through the network (among other things, at layer 3 on the outbound side an "address" gets slapped on the "envelope" which is then read by layer 3 at the destination).
- Layer 2, the *data link* layer, includes flow control of data as they pass down through this layer in one open system and up through the peer layer in the other open system.
- Layer 1, the *physical interface* layer, includes the ways in which data communications equipment is connected mechanically and electrically, and the means by which the data move across those physical connections from layer 1 at the source to layer 1 at the destination.

## WHAT OSI MANAGEMENT IS (OR WILL BE)

OSI Management is a software application of the OSI application layer. Its mission is to manage the *managed objects* (a phrase we'll return to shortly) that represent the OSI layer protocols and the communication services provided by those protocols.

As we stated in Chapter 2, open standards for network management are increasingly important. Why? Because users have an ever-growing need to build, service, expand, and *manage* a reliable and flexible network. These important tasks can't be accomplished efficiently when one NMS is sitting cheek-by-jowl with another one, and each is managing a different proprietary system.

Standards facilitate both choice and integration, and they stimulate a healthy degree of competition among vendors. Standards, it turns out, are not necessarily vanilla.

More specifically, OSI Management standards are being written to specify the software tools needed to monitor, operate, control, and administer layer protocols that provide common communication services to network components in the OSI environment. They define how performance information should be captured and formatted for transfer between open systems. OSI Management provides a common language and protocol specifications that permit NM products manufactured by participating vendors to be able to exchange NM information on a worldwide basis.

This is a critical requirement, because private and public networks around the world are becoming increasingly integrated. If you're not convinced, consider the alternative—proprietary gateways to each network, requiring conversion from one protocol to another at every network interface. This would be costly and inefficient—in short, a mess.

OSI Management has two major uses. First, it can specify the structure of the NM information that is moved from one place to another. Second, it can specify how that information should be transferred from one open system to another.

It is by combining these two uses that OSI Management begins to earn its keep, because that combination allows a *range of functions*. When vendors' NM systems products are finally OSI-conformant, a lot of useful OSI Management functions will become globally available. All vendors' OSI Management-based NMSs will be able to talk to each other. But equally important, users will gain a new measure of control over their networks. For example, they'll be able to specify and constantly redefine the types of information that a particular NMS can send and retrieve. They'll be able to set and change the configurations of, and the relationships among, all managed objects both within and outside a given network.

## WHAT OSI MANAGEMENT ISN'T

Having said all that, it's also important to stress that some things are *not* in the charter of OSI Management.

First, OSI Management isn't one monolithic standard, and it's far from complete. Instead, it's a collection of interrelated standards, which are still in widely varying stages of development. In a subsequent section, we will review the standards that have been completed and some of those that are close to completion.

Second, OSI Management will never be a spec sheet for OSI-based NM systems, or the hardware and software components within the networks that are managed by those systems. In a sense, OSI Management only helps a given NMS walk up to the door of a network, knock on the door, and ask for certain information to be produced according to certain protocols.

OSI Management also says nothing about the graphic interface vendors provide to their clients. Good information goes in and out of the door, but how it presents itself on a screen (or screens) behind the door is not OSI Management's concern.

Finally, although OSI Management attempts to define the broadest range of NM functions, it doesn't suggest that all manufacturers have to offer all of those defined services. OSI Management defines five Specific Management Functional Areas, (SMFAs), which we'll look at in an upcoming section.

Many people have assumed that the creation of standards will lead to a gray and tasteless world of generic NM, where one vendor's NMS will be indistinguishable from another's. Not so! To invoke a sports metaphor: All quarterbacks throw passes and call running plays, but no two quarterbacks manage a team and its resources in quite the same way. In fact, quarterbacks (and NM systems) succeed only to the extent that they combine and execute functions more creatively than their competitors.

## THE FIRST OF THE FULLY BAKED STANDARDS

Like all OSI standards, OSI Management standards go through a lengthy development process of at least four steps: the working document, the committee draft, the draft international standard, and the international standard. Assuming that additional intermediate stages (such as a second committee draft) aren't required, the process of developing a standard generally takes several years of hard committee work. When you consider that more than twenty topics have been agreed on as subjects for standardization, you can see that a great deal of work (more than fifty committee-years) has been required to develop and maintain OSI Management. That's a lot of warm coffee and cold lunches in conference rooms around the world.

On the other hand, the conventional wisdom that OSI Management will *never* fully arrive is wrong. Some standards are already complete, and others are not far behind.

The first full-fledged international standard for OSI Management to be completed was the **OSI Management Framework.** This is a conceptual model, rather than a series of specifications for implementation, but it is nevertheless an extremely important document. Its stated purpose is "to provide a common basis for the coordinated development of management standards"—in other words, to set the stage for all the other standards to come. It has three major components: (1) a definition of the "managed object" within the OSI management world; (2) a description of the three types of "management information exchange"; and (3) an identification of appropriate "specific management functional areas" and "system management functions" in OSI Management.

A **managed object** is just what it sounds like: anything in the network that's available for management. This means a lot more than just devices, such as modems and other communications equipment. It means any "logical representation" of your communications resources—for example, the algorithms that define the parameters of those resources are in fact managed objects. The managed-object category also includes different kinds of network connections (X.25 connections, for example) and protocol entities. This breadth of reference is central, vital, and crucial to OSI Management. Why? Because it begins to define the diverse *characteristics* of a managed object, such as the kinds of operations it can perform, the kinds of information it can send and receive, and its place in the overall cosmology of OSI Management. Unless vendors can agree on the specifications for both the OSI layered protocol entities *and* vendors' communications equipment, the goal of integrated NM will remain elusive.

The OSI Management Framework defines five Specific Management Functional Areas (SMFAs).

figure 5

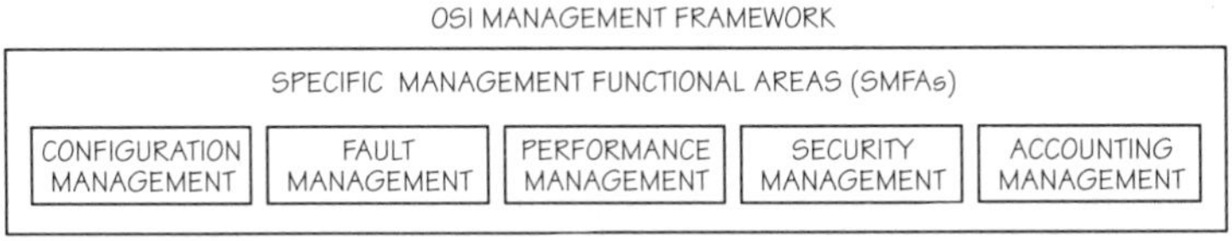

OSI MANAGEMENT FRAMEWORK

| SPECIFIC MANAGEMENT FUNCTIONAL AREAS (SMFAs) | | | | |
|---|---|---|---|---|
| CONFIGURATION MANAGEMENT | FAULT MANAGEMENT | PERFORMANCE MANAGEMENT | SECURITY MANAGEMENT | ACCOUNTING MANAGEMENT |

We won't worry much about the three types of management information exchange (layer management, systems management, and management information in normal OSI-layer protocols). These topics are beyond the scope of this book.

Also defined by the Management Framework are the **Specific Management Functional Areas (SMFAs)**. These are configuration management, fault management, performance management, security management, and accounting management. These functional areas are explicitly specified for the OSI seven-layered protocol entities. Note that they are not standards. However, vendors can and are encouraged to use these functional areas to specify and define the requirements of their own communications equipment.

## SMFAs: SOME MAJOR FUN AREAS

**Configuration management** answers the question, *Where* is everything in my network? This includes information about OSI-layer managed objects, relationships between managed objects, and even relationships between relationships. Configuration itself includes setting network parameters and device thresholds as well as activities intended to control and retrieve information from managed objects in the open system. Although various NMS vendors slice the pie differently, most would include the notions of **inventory management** (keeping track of what's in the system: hardware, software, software revisions, and the like) and **topology manage-**

**ment** (keeping track of how it's all interconnected) under the configuration management umbrella. In the quest for integrated NM, topology management is key.

**Fault management** answers the question, *What* is my network doing? It provides a set of tools, or functions, that identify failures, miscues, and other abnormalities in a network and facilitate correction of these problems. It's the one thing most users would demand from a good NMS: the ability to spot a problem, address the problem, run tests, and keep error logs (also known as *trouble tickets*). And it goes without saying that most users want this function done *quickly.*

**Performance management** answers the question, *How* is my network doing? This functional area provides a set of tools that facilitate gathering statistical data about activity within the OSI environment. Which components in the system are approaching capacity? How quickly are individual components responding to commands? The performance management SMFA ensures a consistent, cross-resource performance measurement and performance history database.

**Security management** answers the question, *Who* is using my network, or more precisely, who is *authorized* to use my network? This SMFA consists of a set of tools designed to protect OSI resources. Put simply, who is authorized to tell a given system to do what, at what time of day, and to what extent?

**Accounting management** answers the question, *When* was my network used, or when is my network being used? It enables the system to notify a user of costs incurred in using OSI resources and also allows accounting limits to be set.

Each SMFA is currently described at length in the OSI Management Framework document drafted by the OSI committee.

## SMFs: STILL MORE FUN

Most SMFAs are supported by one or more beasts called **System Management Functions (SMFs)**. Put differently, when a human network manager wants to perform some task specified by the requirements of SMFAs, that person must in turn specify one or more SMFs.

And, as we'll soon see, the SMF also passes the buck. But first, see Figure 6, a revised version of Figure 5, this time including the SMFs.

Note that there is no direct line drawn between specific SMFAs and SMFs. Suffice it to say that all SMFAs

**Each SMFA calls upon appropriate system management functions for help in carrying out the activities specified in the SMFA.**

figure 6

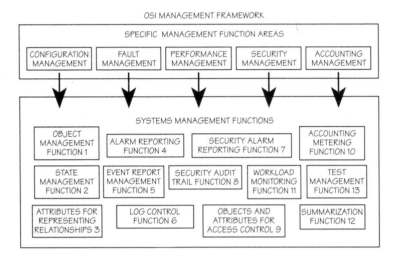

OSI MANAGEMENT FRAMEWORK

SPECIFIC MANAGEMENT FUNCTION AREAS

| CONFIGURATION MANAGEMENT | FAULT MANAGEMENT | PERFORMANCE MANAGEMENT | SECURITY MANAGEMENT | ACCOUNTING MANAGEMENT |

SYSTEMS MANAGEMENT FUNCTIONS

| OBJECT MANAGEMENT FUNCTION 1 | ALARM REPORTING FUNCTION 4 | SECURITY ALARM REPORTING FUNCTION 7 | ACCOUNTING METERING FUNCTION 10 |
| STATE MANAGEMENT FUNCTION 2 | EVENT REPORT MANAGEMENT FUNCTION 5 | SECURITY AUDIT TRAIL FUNCTION 8 | WORKLOAD MONITORING FUNCTION 11 | TEST MANAGEMENT FUNCTION 13 |
| ATTRIBUTES FOR REPRESENTING RELATIONSHIPS 3 | LOG CONTROL FUNCTION 6 | OBJECTS AND ATTRIBUTES FOR ACCESS CONTROL 9 | SUMMARIZATION FUNCTION 12 |

can be used by at least one SMF. Some examples of SMFs include:

- *Object management* initiates various actions to be performed on a managed object.
- *State management* allows a user to monitor the state of objects under management and to receive notices of changes in that state.
- *Attributes for representing relationships* monitors and controls relationships among objects in a system.
- *Alarm reporting* finds, secures, and brings home useful information, particularly in the realm of operational abnormalities.
- *Event report management* allows the user to specify the destination of certain event reports.
- *Log control* enables the user to specify particular events that will be recorded by the system.

- *Test management* enables the user to test and evaluate the state of managed objects.

## CMIS AND CMIP

We have noted that three OSI Management standards have achieved international standard status. In addition to the OSI Management Framework, there are two more recent graduates: the **Common Management Information Services (CMIS)** standard and the **Common Management Information Protocol (CMIP)** standard. In addition to being full-fledged standards, these are our first pronounceable acronyms: "see-miss" and "see-mip."

The system management functions, in turn, invoke required services and protocols of the Common Management Information Services Element (CMISE).

figure 7

Just as SMFs take orders from an SMFA, there is another element that can take orders from an SMF: the **Common Management Information Services Element (CMISE)**—pronounceable as "see-mize." CMISE is simply a combination of the protocols defined by CMIP and the services described by CMIS.

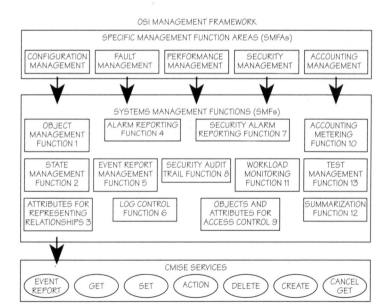

OSI MANAGEMENT FRAMEWORK

| SPECIFIC MANAGEMENT FUNCTION AREAS (SMFAs) | | | | |
|---|---|---|---|---|
| CONFIGURATION MANAGEMENT | FAULT MANAGEMENT | PERFORMANCE MANAGEMENT | SECURITY MANAGEMENT | ACCOUNTING MANAGEMENT |

SYSTEMS MANAGEMENT FUNCTIONS (SMFs)

| OBJECT MANAGEMENT FUNCTION 1 | ALARM REPORTING FUNCTION 4 | SECURITY ALARM REPORTING FUNCTION 7 | ACCOUNTING METERING FUNCTION 10 |
|---|---|---|---|
| STATE MANAGEMENT FUNCTION 2 | EVENT REPORT MANAGEMENT FUNCTION 5 | SECURITY AUDIT TRAIL FUNCTION 8 | WORKLOAD MONITORING FUNCTION 11 | TEST MANAGEMENT FUNCTION 13 |
| ATTRIBUTES FOR REPRESENTING RELATIONSHIPS 3 | LOG CONTROL FUNCTION 6 | OBJECTS AND ATTRIBUTES FOR ACCESS CONTROL 9 | SUMMARIZATION FUNCTION 12 |

CMISE SERVICES

EVENT REPORT   GET   SET   ACTION   DELETE   CREATE   CANCEL GET

Briefly, CMIP is the protocol specification used to move management information between two open systems. In other words, the NMS in one open system can provide instructions and management information to another open system. This transaction takes place between open systems at layer 7 of the OSI Reference Model—the application layer. See Figure 3. CMIP is implemented in an open system by that vendor's **managing process** and **agent process** (we'll see how this works momentarily). This is where competition abounds. For although the CMIP protocol is specified, the managing process and agent process for implementing that protocol will vary from vendor to vendor.

So we've arrived, at long last, at the services themselves. The SMFA uses the SMF, and —as you'll recall—the SMF uses CMISE services. What are those services? Seven straightforward activities, some of which can even be summarized in a simple English syllable: event report, get, set, action, delete, create, and cancel get. See Figure 7.

## A TIE-IT-ALL-TOGETHER EXAMPLE

An example may help clarify the sequence of steps in the system management process. Remember that underlying all this is the OSI Management Framework, the first international standard in this field and an important accomplishment.

All the letters in this example refer to Figure 8. Suppose that some mishap occurs in the context of two open systems at one of the OSI layers in the agent process environment. To return to our ATM example from the beginning of this chapter, suppose that a problem has occurred in one of the managed objects in the ATM system—possibly in a device (such as a modem), or perhaps in a connection (such as an X.25 link). In an ATM network based on and managed according to OSI standards, information is continually moving between these managed objects and the network management system. What follows is an in-depth look at the complex process that results in an alert to the NMS user that there's a problem with an ATM machine at some remote location.

The managed object (A) in the agent process environment sends an event notification (B) to the agent process (C). After processing by the agent process, the event notification is said to be an event report. The event report is sent to the managing process environment using (D) CMIP. The managing process's (E) CMISE services process the event report and pass the results on to (F) the event report function, which in turn passes it on to the human manager user application—(G) the SMFA fault management. The above example illustrates a process initiated by the managed object. However, the CMISE service may also be used by the managing process to get status information from the agent process about the managed object in question. The CMISE service CMIP is used to retrieve status information from the agent process environment.

What's important to remember is that throughout this entire process in both the managing process and agent

**This example shows the managing process at work using the Fault Management SMFA. Note that the process can be initiated by the managed object or the NMS itself. The two-way nature of this management communication distinguishes OSI management from its predecessors.**
figure 8

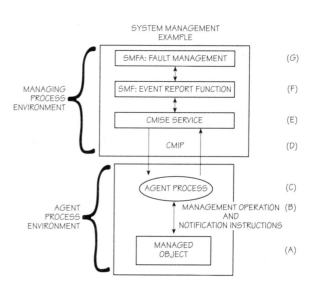

SYSTEM MANAGEMENT
EXAMPLE

MANAGING PROCESS ENVIRONMENT

| SMFA: FAULT MANAGEMENT | (G) |
| SMF: EVENT REPORT FUNCTION | (F) |
| CMISE SERVICE | (E) |
| CMIP | (D) |

AGENT PROCESS ENVIRONMENT

AGENT PROCESS (C)

MANAGEMENT OPERATION (B)
AND
NOTIFICATION INSTRUCTIONS

MANAGED OBJECT (A)

process environments, there is plenty of opportunity for vendors to customize their network management offerings.

And if all these arcane specifics are a bit confusing, perhaps a restatement of some the main points is in order. Basically, in a managed network, a process, once initiated, may result in a response or it may not. (An event report generated by a device and sent in to the manager won't necessarily generate a response from the manager.) Such a process can be initiated either by the managed object or by the NMS itself. It is the two-way nature of this management communication, in part, that distinguishes OSI Management from its more primitive predecessors. In the next chapter, we'll look at some of the desirable NM applications that can be initiated by the NMS.

## RELATED STANDARDS AND INFLUENCES: SNMP AND GOSIP

There are two more related standards you should know about.

In Chapter 2, in the context of SuperManagers, we suggested that there is a wide variety of NM-related protocols, some proprietary, some open. The most important of the nonproprietary NM protocols is **Simple Network Management Protocol (SNMP)**.

SNMP was developed by university researchers as an interim protocol. It is an open standard available to all vendors, permitting some degree of interoperability (particularly on the LAN-management level) until the relevant pieces of OSI Management are ready for implementation. A number of vendors have already incorporated SNMP into their products in the belief that SNMP will be easily convertible to CMIP when the time comes. Other vendors have held back on the assumptions that (1) as OSI Management comes closer to reality, SNMP is likely to be short-lived, and (2) an easy conversion to CMIP is not assured.

The other current influence on standard setting is the **Government OSI Profile (GOSIP**, pronounceable as "gossip.") GOSIP is not a standard in and of itself. Rather, it takes a subset or profile of OSI standards and mandates their adherence in government equipment purchases.

GOSIP is being used by many governments worldwide. Each government, however, can choose the subset of OSI it wishes to implement. Consequently, GOSIP standards will vary from country to country. Currently, an organization of users and vendors known as the OSI Network Management Forum is developing a set of OSI standards profiles called the Open Management Roadmap (OMR). This roadmap contains a series of open management interoperability points call OMNI-Points that can be used by countries around the world to achieve an open management environment.

This may sound circular, but it's important. The U.S. government now requires OSI conformance in a range of network products being sold to the government. Simply put, the federal government wants the ability to hook up communications products from multiple vendors and operate them in a single, transparent, end-to-end-connectable network, and they're using the emerging OSI standards to get there. Down the road, the U.S. government assures us, GOSIP will include precise definitions of how NM systems should communicate with each other and with devices in networks.

And because the U.S. government is the single biggest client for many datacomm and computer vendors, it's safe to assume that GOSIP will have increasing importance in the near term and that integrated NM will develop according to the OSI Management outline. Especially in this case, the client is king.

## OSI MANAGEMENT: SO WHAT?

All of which brings us back to the user, which is where we began our discussion of OSI Management.

We summarized what OSI Management is and isn't. Maybe you'd already heard about the wonders of OSI and were thus surprised to learn that even after it's fully implemented, OSI Management will still leave a lot of NM-related choices to both the manufacturer and the user. OSI conformance will mean conformance in specific areas of OSI management rather than to one unilateral OSI standard. (The ISO is not only responsible for developing OSI standards; they're also charged with developing the test methodologies that vendors will use to *prove* their OSI conformance. So vendors can only claim to be OSI conformant in those areas where they've passed the test.)

"Well, great!"—we can almost hear you saying. "If you'd admitted that before, I could have skipped this chapter altogether. Why make me try to understand something that doesn't exist yet and may not be something you can prove to exist even when it *does* exist?"

The answer is twofold. First, OSI Management will exist, and sooner than many people expect. OSI communications products that implement the ISO's OSI standards (e.g., ISO 8208/CCITT X.25-Packet Layer Protocol [PLP] and ISO 7776/CCITT X.25-Link Access Procedure Balanced [LAPB]) are well established in the marketplace. In the not too distant future, there will be worldwide, one-stop testing for OSI conformance. These OSI communication products are providing common connectivity between different vendors' products. This common connectivity is clearly establishing OSI communication as coming of age.

But just as important—maybe even more important—OSI Management is the first systems network management architecture that reflects the needs of the *user,* as stated by the user. It makes sense, when you think about it. Until the ISO started its work, all distributed communications network architectures were proprietary and all were expressions of a single perspective (that of a computer manufacturer, a common carrier, or whatever). This perspective considered only one architecture (device capability or communication capability). OSI, and OSI Management, on the other hand, have built in the user's perspective (distributed communication and distributed management) from the beginning.

So even if you never hooked your network up to any other network, OSI Management would offer functions that you wouldn't be able to find elsewhere. In short, it's a superior distributed systems management scheme, from the user's point of view, and well worth the wait and the investment.

In Chapter 4, we'll show you how an integrated NMS can take advantage of OSI Management to provide full NM functionality to today's user—and how some of today's systems have already evolved beyond the functionality that OSI Management will finally provide.

# NETWORK MANAGEMENT IN PRACTICE
## OR

*the NMS applies itself*

If you've made your way through Chapter 3 and OSI Management, congratulations. Or if you're taking our suggestion in the preface and are reading Chapter 4 first, welcome. This chapter explains, in untechnical terms, what the most important network management (NM) applications are all about. What does NM accomplish? What's in it for *you*? And, if your company is thinking of adding or upgrading an NM capability, what kinds of questions should you ask potential vendors?

We will be building in several ways on the theoretical worlds described in Chapters 2 and 3. If you've already read those chapters, you'll recognize a lot of the important terminology in this chapter, such as fault management, configuration management, performance management, and so on. We'll be using those same terms, but we'll also be fleshing them out by introducing new concepts.

If you've skipped those chapters, here is network management in a nutshell: NM terminology is evolving quickly and is often general enough to allow a lot of embroidering and interpretation. So when it comes time for you to compare alternative NMSs (network management systems), listen carefully to how applications-related words are being used and make sure you're getting specific enough information to allow you to compare apples to apples.

## BIG NM APPLICATION #1: FAULT MANAGEMENT

Let's begin our discussion of NM applications by sketching two alternative real-life scenarios that describe how a company might use network management to deal with a concrete problem. First, though, we'll admit that the following example is exaggerated, mainly for narrative purposes. It doesn't represent how real network managers spend the bulk of their time, day to day, week to week. But we want to *hook* you first with a cliffhanger and then move on to other equally valuable, but less dramatic, NM activities.

So let's imagine a dynamic Albany-based corporation—call it the Albany Wallbanging Company (AWC)—with a WAN (wide area network) that links Headquarters with a number of regional sales offices in major metropolitan areas around the country. AWC has recently installed an NMS to manage its ever-expanding WAN.

Both of our AWC scenarios begin the same way: One of the company's sales offices is in Pittsburgh. (Lots of walls in Pittsburgh.) Most of the data flowing over the WAN from Pittsburgh to Albany consists of orders—who wants how much wallbanging, and how soon—and most of the information flowing back deals with credit histories, inventories, suggested terms for payment, and so forth. Although Albany and Pittsburgh have their occasional differences, they agree on one thing: this is a very important two-way data flow. Each call and response, to and from Albany, represents money in the bank.

**Scenario #1:** One morning, on the last Friday of a particular month, when history suggests that most of AWC's big Pittsburgh orders will be placed, Pittsburgh finds to its horror that the WAN link to Albany is not performing up to speed. There is, of course, a backup link, but the orders, which as usual are being logged at a dozen customer-rep terminals, are not moving along to Albany as quickly as they should. Pittsburgh, feeling somewhat marooned, places an urgent call to Albany: Help!

**Scenario #2:** One morning, on the Thursday before the last Friday of that same month, AWC's network manager in Albany decides that there's something peculiar about the Pittsburgh-Albany WAN link. On a routine network check conducted during the night, several hours before the first shift arrived, the NMS gathered some data that suggested that Pittsburgh wasn't responding correctly to status inquiries. The link wasn't dead, but it was certainly unreliable.

Scenario #1 describes the reality of most companies that have NMSs. They use their NMSs reactively, either because their system does not allow them to manage proactively or their staff is simply burdened with many other responsibilities. So until that angry call comes in from Pittsburgh (or wherever), little is done to address the problem. Once the problem is acknowledged, the NMS certainly helps in identifying the nature and scope of the situation.

Still, there are three difficulties with this reactive approach to network management:

• The users' needs are probably not being met.
• The corporate investment in NM is not being recovered.
• Vendors are constantly called in to deal with crises, almost guaranteeing that their solutions will be hastily devised and implemented.

Now let's merge our two scenarios into one. On Friday morning, when the panicked call comes in—or on

Thursday morning, when a problem is detected—the process of **fault management** begins. To repeat the plaintive question posed in earlier chapters, What's going *on* out there?

Fault management is the effort to find and fix problems in a network. It usually involves a series of tests, designed to give an ever-more-precise picture of what's going on in the network and thereby to isolate the problem. Sometimes, the problem may be straightforward enough so that detection is easy. For example, the network manager may spot a problem indication on the NM's screen. By stepping through a few more screens, the manager may develop a clear sense of where the network abnormality lies.

This scenario presupposes the existence of some kind of **threshold,** which is an important concept in NM. Obviously, before an NMS can send an indication of trouble (or potential trouble) to the network manager, the system has to know how "trouble" is defined. In many cases, network devices (such as modems) have predetermined performance thresholds and internal testing mechanisms to ensure that the device's performance is satisfactory. This capability can be greatly enhanced by an NMS with its own threshold-setting capabilities, which allow network managers to define "trouble" any way they need to, depending on the changing needs of the network.

Threshold setting also works in reverse. Suppose the network manager doesn't really need to know every time one of the hundreds of leased analog ports drops below a certain predefined performance level. In that case, the manager can simply set a higher threshold, saying, in effect, "Don't call me unless it really gets *bad* out there!"

In any case, the idea is to define potential trouble *before* any real trouble begins. When conditions begin to degrade, your network management system must prove its worth either by fixing problems before a user even knows about them, or by alerting users ahead of time so that downtime can be scheduled.

Some network problems are easily found, defined, and solved. In other cases, the problem may prove more elusive, and more extensive tests may be required. In the NM universe, there are two types of tests: nondisruptive and disruptive. A nondisruptive network test can be run in the background while the normal flow of data continues to move over the circuit being tested, whereas a disruptive test requires a break in the network action.

Generally speaking, the network manager prefers to run disruptive tests in the off-hours. A good NMS can help do that in two ways:

- By *identifying tests as potentially disruptive.* When the manager asks the NMS to run a bit-error rate test on a modem, for example, a screen appears with the caution: "Potentially disruptive test. Do you want to continue?"
- By *offering job-scheduling capabilities,* meaning that disruptive tests can be programmed to run automatically during graveyard shifts, on weekends, or at some other appropriate time.

Given the right NMS, network operators can also take advantage of the system's job-scheduling capability to spot network problems before they become full-blown meltdowns. This approach was described in Scenario #2, above, where AWC's network manager was in the good habit of testing *all* the devices and lines in the network regularly (in this case, sampling network performance every 6 minutes for an hour, every weeknight).

This was not only the result of the manager's natural aversion to disasters. It was also because the proactive manager had chosen a system that would allow determination of which network components were working as well as they were supposed to. For example, AWC had recently purchased a number of high-quality 19.2 Kbps Motorola Codex modems. Wouldn't it make sense to use the NMS's testing capabilities (assuming the NMS *had* these testing capabilities) to see that the modems have been properly installed and are operating as expected? Similarly, why not test the leased phone lines to see if AWC was getting the good lines it was paying for?

Suppose the network manager and a number of the users of the system notice a certain problem over a certain circuit. In response to the manager's inquiry, the telephone company suggests that the problem lies in the modem (or in the NMS, or wherever). The manager doubts it and proceeds to track, for example, the signal-to-noise ratio on that circuit over a week's time. The acceptable level is, say, 24 decibels, but the NMS clearly shows that the actual performance of the line in that week ranges between 18 and 24 decibels. The network manager then presents these data to the telephone company and in a polite tone, asks, "Doesn't this problem belong to you?"

In effect, the network manager is able to take a series of snapshots of the network's performance. These snapshots can be used in many ways—to avoid disasters, to measure how well key corporate assets are performing, and to make underachieving network elements perform properly.

Another aspect of fault management, found in some NMSs, is **trouble ticketing.** Collectively, trouble tickets constitute a library of specific network problems that have arisen, accompanied by their resolution. For maximum usefulness, the library of trouble tickets should be able to be catalogued in several ways, including by:

- Open date or close date
- Site
- Class of device
- Current status (high priority, etc.)

Flexibility in cataloging is an important consideration in an NMS because it guarantees access to information in the library. This is vital information because in a big network environment, you may have hundreds of recorded problems and certain kinds of situations tend to occur repeatedly. Network managers should not have to re-solve the same problems from month to month, day to day, or shift to shift. Trouble ticketing can help avoid this by showing how similar problems have been solved in the past.

As noted in previous chapters, no NMS manages every device that's already in the system. But since trouble ticketing is a *problem* database, it doesn't have to be limited to the subset of network devices managed by a particular NMS. Again, this argues for flexibility. The trouble-ticket form presented by the NMS should be generic enough to capture a core of information about every device in the network. It should also permit the user to append additional kinds of client-specific data (such as test results) to a trouble ticket.

How and why? you may be asking. We've argued that *integration* and an *object-oriented user interface* are characteristics that distinguish a good NMS. Here's where those good qualities find practical application. Suppose the network manager, in searching for problems, is testing one of AWC's Pittsburgh modems. When the NMS focuses on that modem, the system uses its inventory-management function to call up a detailed profile of that device. (More on inventory management below.) The manager decides to save "good data"—meaning bad test results—on a trouble ticket. When the new ticket is called up, the integrated and device-oriented NMS automatically transfers all the relevant information from the general network inventory to the ticket.

As a result, nothing is entered incorrectly. The user doesn't need to record the test or inventory data manually and then reenter it after calling up a trouble ticket. Integration triumphs! And the object-oriented interface means the manager only has to select the device once to access multiple management functions. The system remembers which device it's working on.

Trouble ticketing, as noted, is not found in all NMSs. This example serves to illustrate, once again, the NM will be anything but generic-and-vanilla when universally accepted standards for network management (the subject of Chapter 3) are finally implemented.

## BIG NM APPLICATION #2: PERFORMANCE MANAGEMENT

Fault management overlaps somewhat with **performance management** and other broad NMS-applications categories.

Performance management comprises essentially two groups of activities, which we'll call **snapshots** and **statistics collection**. A **snapshot** in network management is roughly what it is in photography: a single instant in time, frozen and captured to help in detecting faults. It meets the needs of short-term requests (maybe one-time only) for information to try to isolate and identify problems precisely.

**Statistics collection,** on the other hand, occurs over a period of time—for example, by collecting data from tests conducted at 6-minute intervals over an hour. Most systems with this capability can also use these tools to develop a time-lapsed view. For example, the user should be able to ask for reports on a certain device at (for example) 6-minute intervals over 6 months. Ideally, the NMS, which has databased this collected information, can retrieve it at the convenience of the operator and display it in a number of different formats, including both graphical and textual, so it can be used for trend analysis and network planning.

What kinds of information can be collected? All kinds of useful data in critical areas such as (forgive the technobabble) processor loading, link utilization, analog line parameters, EIA signals, and buffer pool utilization.

Analog line performance is a good example. Suppose you're a network manager whose users are complaining of a problem that seems to come up between the same hours every day—say, on a high-speed leased line modem. Sitting down at the keyboard/mouse, you call up a menu of statistics and see which ones you might run on the lines in question. A top-drawer NMS will present you with a range of possible statistics: signal-to-noise, retrains, gain hits, and so on. Then, calling on the job-scheduling function, you can tell the NMS to report on those conditions at a specific time interval.

In addition, certain devices such as some multiplexers and switches gather statistics on how much data they're passing versus their inherent capacity—known in technobabble as the "utilization statistic." The effective NMS can gather these statistics through workload monitoring.

This capability is very useful when the number of endpoints of a network has been increasing while the number of communications devices has stayed the same. The proactive network manager with a good NMS can look backward over, say, the past 6 months, and see almost immediately how network use has changed as new users have been added. With this information in hand, the network manager can estimate when a capacity limit (either of a device's processor or a network link) is being approached. This, in turn, allows the company to consider its options—More lines? More bandwidth through existing equipment? A more powerful switch or multiplexer?—without a sense of impending doom.

This shows that by investing in NM, you're investing in management *tools*. You are attempting to put a collection of assets to their best use at the same time that you're providing an improved (or at least consistent) level of service to end users. Better to provide creative options to management than to battle the notion that you're overseeing some sort of corporate black hole. And better that you call Pittsburgh in a preemptive strike than they call you with desperation in their voices.

## BIG NM APPLICATION #3: CONFIGURATION MANAGEMENT

**Configuration management** involves keeping track of all objects in the network, managed and unmanaged. It also involves controlling and retrieving information from those objects in the network that are managed by the NMS.

In describing the trouble-ticketing procedure, we referred to the **inventory management** database, which stores profiles of all the objects in the network. Together, inventory management (the record of what's in the network) and **topology management** (the record of how it's connected) are the fundamentals of configuration management.

Of course, the record of how it's connected is the result of the actual configuring itself—that is, the actual setting of operating parameters in managed devices as well as the implementation of upload, reconfiguration, time-of-day capabilities, and so forth.

But let's go through these steps one by one.

Depending on the state of a given network, inventorying is a relatively small or a relatively large challenge. If you're just starting to assemble a network—lucky you!—you'll simply have to build in fail-safe control mechanisms to guarantee that every piece of user equipment out there is logged in through the inventory database as it's added. But if your company is typical, with an existing and loosely inventoried network, it will take a large institutional commitment to bring the inventory database up to date.

Nevertheless, we argue, there has to be a single, centralized record of all components in the network, whether managed or unmanaged. Why?

First, to *eliminate confusion.* Ask anybody in the trade: having one or even multiple NMSs for your modems, switches, and multiplexers; a spiral notebook for your terminals; a three-ring binder for your printers; etc.; is the stuff of nightmares.

Second, to *reduce the time required to fix a problem.* Suppose AWC's network manager gets the dreaded call from Pittsburgh: Help! I'm on terminal #5, and nothing's happening! The manager wants to be able to find that terminal fast (inventory management), and see at the same time how it hooks into the network (topology management). It's important to spend less time on establishing connections and more time on trouble-shooting.

There are many ways to represent graphically the information contained in the inventory database. One logical approach is to use a series of increasingly specific and localized views of the network, starting with the largest grouping and working down to the smallest grouping. The largest might be a map of the world, or of one country, with icons representing groups of devices. The next largest might be a region or states within a country; then, as necessary, a series of views all the way down to the building level, or the floor-within-a-building level. Conceivably, the largest view could be of a single building, with other views stepping down from there. But remember that most NM action occurs in the context of WANs spanning geographical distances, and certainly most configuration management takes place in that context.

Ideally, the NMS should have the capability to display many kinds of aggregate pictures (country maps, city-block girds, floorplans, etc.), and should be able to "zoom in" and "zoom out" as needed. Obviously, different businesses need the capability to set up different aggregate views, and some want to create more than one hierarchy of views. A bank, for example, might want to set up separate views of its ATM and accounting networks.

So exactly what happens in configuration management? For example, what happens when a growing company sets up shop in a new location, or an old location begins to use data communications and has to be added to the existing network?

Let's go back to Albany Wallbanging and imagine that AWC is opening a new regional sales office in Atlanta. In Albany, the network manager's job is to enter into the inventory database new devices and lines (the users' terminals, the modem or modems on the users' end, and the relevant transmission lines), and to link them logically to corresponding network devices terminating in Albany, which in turn connect to the host computer. How is this accomplished?

First, the managers must have an NMS with specific types of bells and whistles, as described in the following paragraphs. The network manager first calls up one or more appropriate icons on the inventory management screen, perhaps beginning with the icon for a terminal. This new terminal is located on the appropriate geographic screen—call it Southeast United States—and is given a unique identity. (Most companies develop their own in-house naming systems, keyed to location, technology, or whatever.) The terminal, of course, isn't a managed device—no terminals are—but it is what the user sees, so it makes sense to log it in.

Next, the network manager calls up a managed transmission device icon (say, a modem), and locates the new Atlanta modem, again creating a unique identity for the new device. At this stage of the process, the NMS "knows" that some modems are managed and some are not; and it therefore presents a menu of modems. As soon as the icon for the Atlanta modem is located on the appropriate screen, the manager clicks on a menu entry to identify the *type* of modem for the benefit of the

NMS. As the terminal and modem are added to the inventory, they are automatically registered as either unmanaged or managed, and that distinction is made graphically on the screen.

Next, the network manager tells the NMS how the terminal is connected to the modem. To make this job easier, the NMS provides a picture of all the possible connections (for example, through a data port) from which to make the right selection.

Next, the manager identifies the device to which the Atlanta modem will be linked. It could be directly to Albany, but it's more likely that multiple users in Atlanta will be connected via a "concentration" network—T1, X.25, statistical multiplexing, for example. The NMS also allows the leased line to be named (perhaps with its circuit number as its name), so that in the future, the screen will automatically display the circuit number. The point, again, is to shorten the time needed to resolve problems. (As explained in Chapter 1, the good NMS promotes high network availability while it's saving money.) Once the managed object is connected and named, a truly useful NMS will be able to help fill the database: inventory and configuration uploads will extract information directly from the device and enter it into the database.

Finally, the network manager locates the new Atlanta devices in the macro-to-micro hierarchy of views of AWC contained in the NMS. Perhaps Atlanta becomes a new system node, with its own aggregate icon in the United States or world maps. If so, then all the recently defined devices and lines get housed, logically, under this new node icon.

Like trouble tickets, inventory screens should include fields for both generic and company-specific information. This sort of housekeeping is actually exciting when you consider how vital a resource it is. Right at your fingertips is everything you need to know. Who installed the device? When? Who should get the call if there's a problem?

And there's more. For example, most networks get to the point at which it would be helpful to change the configuration of specific devices within them, whether to solve a problem, avoid a problem, or improve performance. Today, some NMSs are able to take on this task, while others are not.

Suppose, for example, that a given network node suffers some sort of catastrophe, which results in a loss of memory. With a proactive configuration-management function, configuration records can be down-line loaded—to return to our first example, from Albany to Pittsburgh—to the malfunctioning node. This jumpstarts Pittsburgh without requiring skilled technical people from Albany to be on site.

More proactively, the network manager can define multiple alternative configurations to vary the operation of the network for different situations or times of day. These alternative configurations can be activated automatically to run at a specific time. For instance, maybe AWC does the payroll every Thursday, and large volumes of data need to be dumped off in the process of cutting checks. In that case, the network manager— given a little patience and a high-quality NMS—can set up a "Thursday afternoon" configuration, prioritizing traffic for the terminals and printers over in Payroll.

Configuration management is a realm in which competition will be intense in the coming years, as various vendors of NMS seek to win the hearts and minds of increasingly sophisticated NM consumers. Entirely aside from price considerations, the best NMS would actively manage the entire universe of devices, and manage them all down to the level of configuring their operating characteristics. But, as noted at the outset, no system does this today—and even if one did, few companies could justify paying the price it would have to command.

It's certainly fair, however, to say that some vendors and their respective NMSs are more flexible than others. So when in doubt, *ask*. Ask what range of devices a proposed NMS can manage. And, within that range, ask what devices the NMS can reconfigure from a central location. And if you aren't satisfied, ask again. Announce that you want to go over it all one more time, but nice and *slowly* this time.

# OTHER VALUE-ADDED NM APPLICATIONS

OK, so now we've hooked you, through the tales of Albany Wallbanging, and we can move on to some quieter (but still vital) NMS functions: accounting management and security management. Together they represent the administrative, planning, and control functions of an effective NMS and can therefore be a key value-added feature of such a system.

**Accounting management** facilitates the centralized management of customer use of the network—for example, in circumstances like X.25 or dial applications, where users are billed for services over networks. It enables a company to capture statistics about the usage of the network in forms that can generate various kinds of reports.

The variety of approaches to report generation through accounting management is infinite. The spectrum ranges from the standard-but-simple report that may be provided in the NMS software package and which can be run on-line, to much more elaborate kinds of reports that demand specialized programming and ongoing attention. For example, Company A may only ask its NMS to provide a preprogrammed configuration report at a specific interval. Company B, by contrast, may have a separate reporting center that combines the power of the NMS with specialized software and mainframe computing capabilities.

Reports can be very specific. Earlier, we talked about collecting network performance statistics. These have value as planning tools. For example, a company may have recently invested in a new and expensive line of modems, and—facing further expansion—may want to know whether that was a smart investment. The good NMS is able to generate any number of reports on the performance of those modems over almost any specified time period. For example: How many high-level alarms came in during peak traffic hours at the end of the billing cycle?

**Security management,** our second low-profile but high-return function, involves the creation and monitoring of various network security mechanisms. What's critical here is to distinguish between network security and the security of the NMS itself.

First, some general thoughts about network security. It's worth remembering that most of the time, NM data and user data travel along separate routes. At times, the two data streams travel in separate channels along the same path; at other times, they travel over literally separate cables.

Logically, then, NM data either: (1) are isolated from user data and meaningless to the outsider; or (2) are tucked into the main data channel, are just as well protected as that main channel, and are still meaningless to any network intruder who might show up on the electronic doorstep. (In the second case, NM data can be interwoven with any kind of data, whether those data are encrypted or nonencrypted.) In short, if a company's user data aren't secure *before* the addition of the NMS, they won't be more secure afterward. Conversely, the addition of an NMS can't make user data less secure. The addition of an NMS to an existing network, in other words, doesn't create a new security exposure beyond the obvious facts that NM functions (but *not* user data) are now (1) centralized, and (2) reasonably comprehensible to the inquiring mind.

Before looking at specific security-management issues, let's look at the NMS itself as a focus of security. This theme can be summarized in two points:

- First, as already noted, the network management database that captures your network—from the NMS itself to the farthest reaches of your empire, even including the passwords used to access certain devices or applications—represents a large corporate investment. It follows that this big investment, once made, deserves to be protected.
- Second, because a sophisticated NMS has significant power over certain functions of the network, it has to be protected against unauthorized and accidental intrusions.

Having stated the obvious, let's look at how security management can be a proactive tool in the hands of the network manager.

First, overall access to the network and its components can be fine-tuned by means of a good NMS. For example, perhaps your company feels that new users, the night shift, or some other subset of users should have read-only access to certain files. This can be programmed into the network by the NMS, keyed either to specific terminals, specific user passwords, or times of day.

Security management can also control specific NM applications. For example, your company may decide that certain NMS operators should be empowered to change the configuration of specific devices but not empowered to add or delete devices or to execute disruptive tests.

Security management can be used to *segment* the computer resource within a company. Perhaps your company has two major divisions—say, East Coast and West Coast. Security management lets those divisions review but not edit each other's work.

To sum up, security management, like accounting management, has great potential as a productive application of network management. But two resources are needed, in order for that potential to be realized: (1) creative users, and (2) a flexible and integrated NMS.

## THE PUNCH LINE

Note that in that last sentence, we slipped "creative users" in ahead of the high-power NMS. This may atone for our overall bias in previous chapters—toward technology, and away from the people who *use* the technology. We hope you'll agree that this is an understandable bias, when one's task is reviewing a sophisticated technology. Nevertheless, it's time to consider a few of the human aspects of NMS.

At the beginning of this chapter, we outlined two scenarios: one in which the Albany Wallbanging Company has an NMS but was only able to use it reactively; and a second in which AWC, in the person of its network manager was proactively using its NMS. Obviously, both Albany and Pittsburgh were better off when the second, more proactive scenario was played out.

Now it can be told: we asserted earlier that the best NMS in the world is only as useful as its users make it. But it's also only as useful as its *manufacturers* make it.

In other words, we're arguing for user friendliness and real integration in network management systems. And this is the second-to-last test to which you should put a proposed NMS. *Look* at the thing. See how it presents its information to the user. Is this system going to get turned on and treasured? If not, keep looking.

We submit, for example, that a good NMS *has* to be a user-friendly NMS. This argues (in our minds) for a user interface that is graphical and menu-oriented rather than syntax driven.

The advantages of such an approach are numerous. First, a graphically oriented control language is likely to be accessible to a relatively wide range of users. (Perhaps less skilled operators can be hired for some applications; or perhaps a long-overdue technological consolidation can be implemented; or perhaps the company will simply be more open to trying out new technologies in the network.)

Second, it tends to ensure that once a single application is mastered—say, device configuration—other applications are likely to follow fairly easily. Comfort and confidence levels are high; technophobia is low. (This is not to say that graphics are always better. Certain highly skilled operators prefer to speed things up by using a command language, perhaps with scripting or macro commands. A flexible NMS would provide this capability as well as graphics.)

The last test that we'd propose is a related one: Is the company *behind* the proposed NMS user friendly? Does the proposed vendor offer the kind of service— both in terms of startup and maintenance—that you anticipate needing? Again, look for a vendor who lets you say yes to this very important question.

## A LAST GRAND EXAMPLE

Just how does your (high-performance, user-friendly, integrated) NMS fit into a large, complex wide area network?

Figure 9 diagrams a private voice and data network in what could be a typical manufacturing application. It's basically an X.25 network with a T1 backbone, all managed from the Chicago central site. The data carried between headquarters and remote offices include inventory, shipping, sales, and pricing information. The

*Here, a worldwide network is managed from a central site; the NMS provides visibility of the entire network, from headquarters to remote locations.*

product is warehoused at the Atlanta site. The bandwidth afforded by the T1s will support voice as well as data. The PADs can handle SDLC and X.25 protocols. The X.25 packet switched data network (PSDN) provides international communications with European distributors based in Paris.

**figure 9**

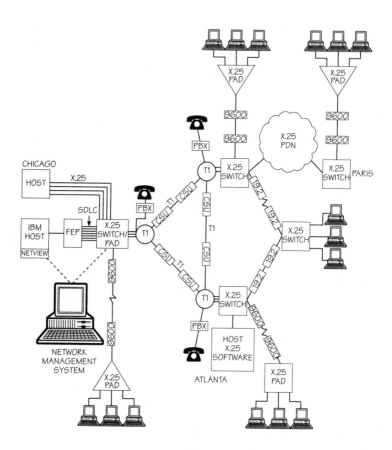

In terms of vendor equipment and diverse technologies, this looks like the proverbial three-ring circus. Yet the network manager has assembled the best technologies for these particular applications. And from the network management console, our user has end-to-end visibility of the entire network from the Chicago headquarters to the remote nodes. Any problems can be monitored, diagnosed, and often remedied without remote on-site intervention. Network availability is maximized, the business enjoys nonstop communications, and this, after all, is what information networking is all about.

So now you know most of what you need to know about NM and NMSs. And because network management is, at heart, a very logical activity, common-sense questions will take you the rest of the way.

# INDEX